PRAISE FOR GHOST :: SEEDS

"Sebastian Merrill's *GHOST :: SEEDS* sings into a rich tradition of trans poetics while also charting its own unprecedented course through the wilds of history, myth, nature. In one poem, he writes, 'If Spring comes, / I will know // my name.' In another, 'Yet always I feel you tight within, / a second heartbeat / inside my chest.' Merrill is the rare emerging poet who possesses not just an urgent narrative, but also the unmistakable lyric and psychospiritual maturity to render that narrative into unforgettable poems that will illuminate and usefully complicate the lives of its readers. *GHOST :: SEEDS* announces the arrival of an important new voice in American poetry."

—**Kaveh Akbar**, author of *Martyr!*

"*GHOST :: SEEDS* testifies to poetry's ability to make meaning of experience, to render experience into language, and to gather time, space, feelings and thought and give those elements an artful home. Before Sebastian Merrill wrote this remarkable book, we did not have this thrilling lyrical narrative of trans experience braided into myth, in which the orphic poet transits into the underworld to encounter his former self. Here, however, the myth is more than a story; it is a narrative newly arrived in our contemporary context, placed on the rocky shores of Maine, dealt with in a 21st century world of vivid, liberating self-realization. *GHOST :: SEEDS* is a moving, nuanced, and memorable book, and one of the most exciting debuts I've read in years."

—**Mark Wunderlich**, author of *God of Nothingness*

"The joy of the body, the dream of the body, the myth of the body, the making. I just love this book in all its embodiments. Can a book of poems see me? It feels like this book does, in the way it marks the history of how many selves one body can hold and how history is the slipperiest part that never leaves us. How do we make peace with what is left behind in the luminous journey to become our deepest truth. What does lineage mean? What is home? In this book the land welcomes and makes a path for the bodily vessel: a kind of pedagogy the earth and the water gives us. I feel so deeply indebted to the joy, grief and, generosity of this formally and psychically rigorous book. How astonishing ordinary life is. And how hard won."

—**Gabrielle Calvocoressi**, author of *Rocket Fanta*

T0283800

PRAISE FOR GHOST :: SEEDS

"Every poem happens in the body, yes, but the poems in Sebastian Merrill's *GHOST :: SEEDS* are doubly embodied. This collection foregrounds the somatic nature of poetry's choreographed language in order to make flesh an emergent speaking self who cherishes his hard-won existence. Like a muscular dancer whose soft landings turn effort to grace, these poems handle the weightiest concerns with a lightness of touch that amazed me across the book. I need a new word to name the emotion evoked by the lucid palimpsest of transformations Merrill enacts in this celebration of what can only come into being by letting go of what was—or by holding what was, even when it's gone. Every poem is this stunning debut is an alchemical swirl of eye, ear, tongue, and lung. These poems made me breathe deeper."

—**Jason Schneiderman**, author of *Hold Me Tight*

"In Sebastian Merrill's collection *GHOST :: SEEDS*, there is the gorgeous clarity of the crossing—the 'trans-'—as much as there is an abiding haziness by that self and certainly by others. And, for this reader, there is a haunting sense that I have experienced my own version of that dynamic. The speaker's realizations emerge in large part through an insistent play with language. From the first poem, the point of view is plural: me with My man's name and you '(my ghost),' Girl-ghost, inverted twin, lost sister. At times, Gender is embodied: my Gender wanders in the underworld. At other times, the 'you' enters into a sequence 'Ghost :: Persephone' where the you is an interpretation of Persephone who can tell their singular story. A moment of kayaking, for instance, is set against this backdrop and yet Merrill doesn't retell the myth so much as use it as touchstone. What is missed, found, mourned, and celebrated is a reason for celebration. Thank you, Sebastian Merrill."

—**Kimiko Hahn**, author of *Foreign Bodies*, and final judge

GHOST :: SEEDS

Poems

Library of Congress Cataloging-in-Publication Data

Names: Merrill, Sebastian, author.
Title: Ghost :: seeds : poems / Sebastian Merrill.
Description: First edition. | Huntsville, Texas : TRP: The University Press
   of SHSU, [2023]
Identifiers: LCCN 2023014105 (print) | LCCN 2023014106 (ebook) | ISBN
   9781680033519 (paperback) | ISBN 9781680033526 (ebook)
Subjects: LCSH: Persephone (Greek deity)--Poetry. | Transgender
   men--Poetry. | Gender identity--Poetry. | Ghosts--Poetry. | LCGFT: Queer
   poetry. | Fantasy poetry.
Classification: LCC PS3613.E7764 G48 2023 (print) | LCC PS3613.E7764
   (ebook) | DDC 811/.6--dc23/eng/20230421
LC record available at https://lccn.loc.gov/2023014105
LC ebook record available at https://lccn.loc.gov/2023014106

Cover design by Zoe Schlacter

Printed and bound in the United States of America

Published by TRP: The University Press of SHSU
Huntsville, Texas 77341
texasreviewpress.org

GHOST :: SEEDS

Poems

Sebastian Merrill

TRP: The University Press of SHSU
Huntsville, Texas

TABLE OF CONTENTS

For Dane.

Girl-ghost.

You bloom in the air

        when our father utters
    the half-halted phrase of your name,
                    the exhalation of *ha*—
cut off by a quick revision to my name.

                My man's name.

    You shimmer in pronouns,

        in the half-said *shhhh* of she, in the red
    edge of *her* slipping
                    into the sibilance of *his*.

When our father calls me   *sweetie* or *honey*,
        it's not me he calls to
                    it's you.

            you (myself)

    you (my lost)

                you (my ghost)

Inverse twin, lost sister,

like our dead, you live in memory:

our grandmother's clouded eyes
        saw you instead of me. In the cold,
                my bones still ache along your long-healed

                        fractures. I've spent years distancing myself
                from you, but here, in our grandparents' home,
        I want to pull you close. When the spring

snows melted, I left my apartment in the city,
        headed north through twisting back roads
                over mountains, stopped to pee, squatting

                        behind bushes, until finally I arrived here,
                on this Maine island. The cottage still
        overlooks the rocky coast. Every dawn,

I paddle through the wind-whipped waves
        of the Thread of Life ledges, those jagged
                rocks the seals love. I find wonder

                        even in the swirls of floating plastic:
                deflated balloons, grocery bags, forlorn
        shoes. Do you remember the summers

we spent here? The swimming lessons
        in the frigid water, the sea stars
                in the tidal pools?

                        My grief for our grandparents
                has grown without you. Also,
        all the sea stars have disappeared.

Where do we converge,

overlay each other

like a poorly developed film,

our two images a blur of light and form?

Where and when

do we divide?

Every Sunday I pierce my thigh
    with the silver fish of a needle.

        Is this what separates me
          from you?

I inject testosterone synthesized in a laboratory,
    made from soybean and yams.

        Like magic, it's difficult to believe
          this exhilaration of hair

           on my face and chest
           comes from plants.

        When I thief myself out,
I am halted by mirrors: this beard

           that grows miraculous
            and strange.

Or did our separation begin before
the needle,
with the surge of curves,

moon-pull
of your period: bright
unwelcome blood?

Is this body what pulled us apart?

Small comfort I found

learning to hate your body
just as other women learned

to hate their bodies.

And even though I could list
     the changes I have made to, as   they

       say, *confirm my gender*,

    to explain how I came out of   you,
      how you became   me,

        this is not our
          story.

This is not the story I want to tell of   us.

If our mother were to tell our story,
        it would begin with grief.

            She mourned your loss,
                her only daughter.

        How could I comfort her
            for the loss of you?

                The loss of you   who is also me.

                I wanted to be her world's center.

We are still the same one child,
            all of you is also all of me.

                        I am her only son.

                        This frame of grief feels inaccurate.

                                Incomplete.

Our father would begin with God.

Angry in his fear,
he wrote you letters.

Messages I could hardly bear to read.

Something about Christ.

Something about the Virgin Mary, that holy vessel.

Something about sacrifice.

my Gender floats on salt

my Gender transcends time

folds into myth

flows gentle beneath the earth

my Gender has a forgotten name

my Gender yowls

is wrapped in grief

my Gender is a plucked rose

a ghost

my Gender wanders in the underworld

my Gender is a full moon

a spring-born seal pup

my Gender is evergreen

my Gender mirrors and twins

glows like a firefly

my Gender haunts

my Gender sings

alights

I think of Persephone:

torn between two worlds, hidden
        beneath the earth.

            Both alive   and dead.

        Stolen from herself, estranged.

I like to imagine you
        as an underground goddess.

            Lost, yes.

        But also powerful, unaged.

Would you begin

    with our separation

        from one whole self into two,

    the man that is me,

        and the residual you?

Or would it begin with our birth:

        a difficult pregnancy,

    our father's surprise when we were born a girl.

        He had wanted to name us John,

    after himself, and our grandfather, and our great-grandfather,

        a long line of fathers with the same name

            reaching back to the 16th century.

        Is ours the story of a family

            breaking?

Ghost :: Persephone

Tied though I may be to the dark
hold of the earth, let me speak:

my story is not yet complete.
My path sluices through granite

and limestone, into caverns
of water and night. You imagine me

as Persephone: I am her. And more.
Stuck, like her, beneath the world

you see, overshadowed
by a mother's grief. Sometimes,

I feel it too—the sting of loss,
all that I could have been.

But here, in the deep recesses
of stone, out of sight

of stars and green, I will seek
a heaven all to myself.

I will learn to sing.

Persephone, I'm afraid.

I'm afraid to speak   your true name aloud

or even to write it down.

It's not that I don't love you—

It's just that your name, my first,
has been used too often
to obscure me.

I could say your name is dead.

If I voice your name
will you superimpose yourself
over me?

If you solidify, become more clear,
will I turn transparent?

Will I disappear?

Ghost :: Persephone

It is always night

in the underland.
I rarely dream.

I reach the cliff

of my longing amid
the press of stone

and dark. No sky,

no fall I can plummet
that will not land me

back where I began,

in these caves
alit by glowworms,

cut through by the river.

I miss the thrum of the world
above, the mountain-spring

of our mother's voice.

I remember everything:
the sea stars, the pines,

the whirl of the Milky Way,

staying up all night
just to see the sun rise.

I wake up before dawn, launch
     my kayak with the sun, paddle out
         along the island's windward side.

         The cliffs glow rosy in the early
     light. I survey the coast, the wall
of seemingly impenetrable rock,

searching for the dark aperture
     of the sea cave I found last summer.
         I hear it first, the sea's surge

         through the narrow opening.
     The tide is right, my boat
slim enough to fit, so I surf

in on the swell through the black
     mouth into a cavern of glistening
         stone. The sea swirls around me,

         echoes. Light filters in, illuminates
     the vast space. Overhead, a rustle
of bats. An in-between space, this

surprise of air within the press
     of earth and water. Across from
         the entrance, the curve of stone

         squeezes into a dark tunnel.
     If I could follow this river
into the earth, would it lead

me to you, your underworld?
     I backpaddle away from the close,
         too tight to fit even my narrow hull.

         The air sucks in and out,
           a giant's breath.

your Gender is a punk house party

with one hundred bikes locked to the chain link fence outside

your Gender is Peter Pan

your Gender is a succulent in a pot the color of fresh turmeric

your Gender is a wet dog

your Gender smells like a lavandin and patchouli candle

a waft of warm buckwheat

your Gender is an egg hatching

that first tap and crack

your Gender is a kiss goodnight

the click of a light

an electric razor buzz

your Gender is a kindergarten portrait in a sea-foam green stegosaurus frame

a ceramic harbor seal with a cracked left flipper and a goofy grin

your Gender is an exclamation point

an aquamarine crystal

your Gender is sponsored by the color pink

please wait

your Gender is not in our database

This house is a time machine.

Our images are still
affixed to the fridge by rusty magnets,

held within dusty photo albums.

A rolodex on the coffee table spins to

your wide smile shining with braces,
hair messily braided,
our one body
frilled in a dress.

Despite years of orthodontics, the space
between your two front teeth never closed.

Our two front teeth?
Your braces.
My gap.

Remember that dress, the scratch
of ruffles,

our young voice lifting
into high soprano.

Bound by rocky headlands,
        this northern coast is hard
              and sharp: few beaches

                    greet the pounding surf.
        I paddle through an ocean
studded with islands,

each a small world in itself:
        Birch Island frames Little Harbor,
              the sheltered waters home to herons,

                    cormorants, and eiders;
        Hay Island holds two hand-hewn
houses; ospreys nest on the tip

of Crow Island. I gentle my speed
        through the Thread of Life, watch
              the spring-born seal pups swim

                    fearlessly alongside their cautious
        mothers. After paddling through the Thread,
I land on Thrumcap Island's rare beach.

At high tide, the water shines
        turquoise above the creamy sand,
              a mix of stone and crushed shells:

                    oysters, whelk, blue mussels,
        snails, and clams. I carry my boat
high above the reaching waves,

tear off my shirt, dive
        into the relentless sea.

Buoyed by the salt water,
        I float weightless and free
                until I no longer feel

                      the cold. I emerge goose
            pimpled, lie on the sand
      to soak in the sun. As I drift

toward sleep, a woman paddles
        onto the beach. I recognize
                her face, even though we

                      haven't seen her for ten years
            at least. You used to play
      kick-the-can with her

and the other island girls.
        She doesn't know me
                at first, and nervous, shy,

                      I don't offer a greeting.
            Until, with a flicker, she sees
      you within me. *Is it you?* she asks.

I stand up fast, nod, cross
        my arms over my scarred,
                flat chest. It's confusing,

                      introducing myself
            to someone you knew.
      But she's friendly enough,

so we stand in the surf
        and watch the gulls wheel
                over the churning waves.

Here   in this one place

          both   you and I   have lived,

you luster, flash

                    bright.

          I branch   away from you

                    then back then

                              away.

Tell me

          am I the fig

                                        and you   the wasp?

                              Am I sound   and you Echo?

          Am I   the pomegranate

          and you

                    the seed?

Ghost :: Persephone

The inky black of the mantilla
I wrap over my shoulders hides

my own strength, my tensed
muscles. The lace whose blackness

is pinpricked, starry, like a memory
of the night sky. Shut as a seashell,

I have become hard and savage.
I play hopscotch with death, sing

a dirge for the woman I could have
been. I keep searching

for some kind of definition.

You used to love

       flipping through the pages
       of the Oxford English Dictionary,

would always head straight
            for the heavy tome
     in the library:

          the etymologies and definitions
              a comfort in their assuredness,
                 their seeming solidity.

      Now I click through the OED online,
        scroll through words.

I look up *gender*, delight
     in obsolete definitions—

Gender :: seeds

Gender :: frame

Gender :: scene

Gender :: play

Gender :: power

Gender :: chest

Gender :: drag

Gender :: lash

Gender :: nail

Gender :: teeth

Gender :: edge

Gender :: balm

Gender :: flight

Gender :: tease

this :: Gender :: is not your home :: ! ::

Gender :: needle

Gender :: pill

Gender :: knife

I am hesitant to speak
of surgery, even to you.

This one change.

I had ceased to be you
even before I submitted
to the surgeon's knife.

There was no one moment of separation,
instead, many:

my nascent becoming,

the needle, the knife,

later, our legal division.

I hid the documentation
in the top drawer of my dresser,
buried beneath a book
of stamps, a butt plug,
our grandfather's ring, some old letters.

I built a fence in my mind around the lost sound of your name.

Years later, while watching a movie, a friend asked,
Does it feel strange that the main character has your dead name?

I hadn't even noticed.

It was as if you had disappeared.

You weren't there and then

as bees from a hive,

a swarm of sting and honey,

you emerged.

Ghost :: Persephone

I name each day

as my own, find

forgetting

the tang of grief

takes time.

Look:

a pomegranate

is a world

I can burst open.

As I pluck each

ruby seed, I repeat

my golden name.

My voice reverberates

off the cave walls,

echoes out over

the still waters

of the lake.

I find comfort in the rhythm
      of the tide's twice-daily cycle,
            covering then revealing

                over ten feet of snails and seaweed,
          slippery rock. This long, slow breath
      a constant reminder of the moon's

pull, that no transition occurs
      in pure isolation. It's easier
           to carry my kayak to the water

                when the tide is high. I cinch tight
          my life vest before I launch.
      The snug hold around my chest

reminds me of binding: the ache
      of my back, my tight breath.
           I wound muslin over and over

                your breasts, tried ACE bandages,
          duct tape, compression binders,
      learned how to hide your body

so I might be seen. I turned
      away from you—

      I had to.

By mid-summer, lobster buoys
        dot the water's surface, a collection
                of distinct patterns: flamingo

                        pink with lime green polka-dots,
                mandarin orange with butter yellow
        stripes. Paddling out, I think

not of the working traps
        tethered to the air by
                braided nylon lines,

                        hauled up every few days
                by the lobstermen who empty
        out their precious catch,

but of the ghost traps,
        cut off from their umbilici,
                lost over the years

                        to storms, boat propellers,
                vindictive rival fishermen.
        Abandoned on the seabed,

they continue to capture
        lobsters, rock crabs, sea bass.
                For years unseen, they green

                        with seaweed and algae,
                are studded with barnacles,
        slowly rust in the corrosive

salt, sink into the ooze
        of mud, become bizarre
                synthetic beasts devouring

                        without mind, without
                        reason.

dig a hole for your Gender

in dirt mud   sand

stretch out your Gender like an elastic band

tie your Gender to a balloon—let it fly

dive your Gender under the sea

hide your Gender in a drawer

fuck your Gender into a lover

pour your Gender into your tea

wash your Gender with soap and water

invite your Gender on a date

allow your Gender to curl up on your bed

massage your Gender into your skin

listen to your Gender patter with the rain

bury your Gender in the underland

meet your Gender on a moonless night

unlock your Gender with this key

sing with your Gender in the shower

own your Gender

or set your Gender free

Ghost :: Persephone

You and I both know
Persephone was just a person
trapped in the amber
of one greedy mistake.
It's a poor parallel, the thread
you've needled between her
and me. Our longest grief
hangs within what's unsaid:
a cool blue current
I don't have the strength
to swim against. Instead,
I perch within brackets.
It can be difficult to disentangle
metaphor from myth,
girl from ghost,
my mothwing life
from the rush of the river
flowing to the changeable sea.
To find me, you must not turn
back, you must not leave.
Paddle your little boat out
through the surf, follow the coast
to the sea cave, this one hidden
entrance to my underworld.
Squeeze your boat through
the stone's pinch, bend your body
nearly double to enter
this deep earth.
Though you may scrape
your knuckles bloody
against the rough rock,
do not retreat. Follow
the river until the tunnel
widens and you can sit up
and breathe—taste of salt,
seaweed, a whiff of smoke.
It takes a long time
for the eyes to adjust
to the enfolding dark.

I paddle through the Thread
        of Life back to Thrumcap.
                A rank stench hits me

                        before I land. A form lies
                bloody on the seashell sand.
        Slashes rend across mottled grey

fur, a mouth gapes wide: razor
        edge of pointy teeth. I move
                closer until the image resolves

                        into a dead harbor seal, beached.
                Was it carried in by the tide? Struck
        by a speeding boat? Victim

of a shark attack? Death here
        feels wrong. I use the flood
                tide to float the torn body

                        back out to sea. After, I can't
                eat the sandwich I brought,
        nor the ripe peach. I turn

towards home with the tide,
        flanked by seals: their eyes
                follow me as they inhale

                        deep pulling breaths
                before slipping back
        beneath the waves.

You could ask,
  When did you realize you were trans?

Which is another way of asking *When did you realize you were not me?*

  There was no one moment. Instead,
    there was a ripple. A flat stone

     skipped over calm

       water, a surfacing

    of desire. Then, a sinking down

     to the bottom.

Harbor seals can dive to depths of five hundred feet,

                  remain submerged for up to thirty minutes.

            On a deep dive, their heart rate slows down

                  to just three or four beats a minute.

      After surfacing, their heart rate speeds up, flutters faster.

            I didn't emerge for years.

          When I finally lifted up to the light,

            it was a kind of deep stretching,   a pulling apart
                    of the fascia that wove us together

        until I had removed even your name
                  from my legal record.

But still I wonder,

     how toned a chest, how thick a beard, how much T do I need?

     What does it mean to be a man?

     What does it mean to be me?

Ghost :: Persephone

I have no answers.
I possess a tongue, maps,
night. Am I an arrow

from hell? An impossible
bending spoon? Estranged
in this new knowledge

of the earth and the starless
rivers that run beneath,
I can no longer return

to how I was before.
You swear that without me,
winter. But did I choose to hide

the sun from the sky?
Frozen, the ground cracks
with questions. I am still

tossing, pulled between two
worlds. It's hard to believe
this same sun still rises even

after we were ripped apart.

find your Gender   inside a pinata

inside a balloon

a matryoshka doll

eject your Gender out of a paint gun

bite into this cupcake to discover your Gender

light this candle

scratch off this card

your Gender will be seen   in a smoke bomb

in the burnout from a race car

in the flash of a lightsaber

in the changing colors of a dragon egg

launch your Gender with a confetti cannon

your Gender is in   an old wives' tale

fingernail polish

a locked box

fireworks will burst your Gender into the night sky

pull your Gender like a rabbit out of a hat

A dense fog descends,
        obscures the sun, heavies
                the air. Moisture condenses

                        on the almost-intangible
                spider webs lacing the pine
        boughs. Only the edge

of the ocean is visible: waves
        emerge as small miracles
                of motion and sound

                        from the obliterating
                                whiteness.

Three thousand
        miles away, a wildfire rages.

        At a gender reveal party,
    expectant parents tried to display
                sex in colored smoke.

                        Sparks flew, igniting
                dry grass. The blaze screamed
        out wide—

                        I scroll through photos of the orange sky.

The ash and smoke drift east,
        replacing the fog to shroud
                even the sun I see.

Did our division begin
                with the discovery of my name?

                        Acting as Sebastian
                in a college production of *Twelfth Night*,
                                the name felt right.

        One night, after rehearsal, I told our friends,

                Call me Sebastian, even when I'm not on the stage.

        Over ten years since I found my name,
                I'm still emerging:

                        I grow my hair long for the first time
                                since I abandoned you.

        I buy pink shorts from the women's department,
                                pierce my septum.

                        Our grandmother taught you how to knit;
                        I teach myself how to cable,
                        follow her pattern for socks.

                        Sometimes I even miss
                                your nipples, your breasts,
                                their ability to feel a tender caress,
                                the slightly sweet smell they left
                                        in the cups of your bra.

I always seem to come back to the body,
          this frame that houses my *I*.

    These past ten years, I've shaped myself
                  into the form I always wanted,

      the body I secretly coveted
          when I was still hidden within you.

Think evergreen.

    Think shell.

      Think dive.

                Dive.

Drop.

            The open sea.

I paddle five miles out, through
            the Thread, past Thrumcap,
                    beyond the roil of the Bulldog

                        off Inner Heron Island.
                Near the Hypocrites, I spot
        a spout, then another: porpoises

crest the waves. I increase
        my speed, try to keep up
                with their swift dash—

                    I follow them all the way
                to Ram Island, where I pause
        to rest, watch them swim

onward toward the horizon.
        I pull my kayak up a ramp
                slick with seaweed, then

                    climb onto a granite pier
                overlooking the narrow harbor.
        I bend my knees, spring

up into the air, swing
        my arms overhead to avoid
                the water's bright slap.

Ghost :: Persephone

When I want to feel
weightless

I dive into the river,
allow my heavy body

to slacken, cradled
by the lightless water.

If spring comes
I will know

my name,
follow the tunnel

bitten through
the hard earth, lose all

dignity as I leap
to the upward sky.

My life has become
an upside-down cup:

what sad water I've found
in this buried river,

these eyeless fish, sulfurous
depths. I am a singer

without rain, skyless.
I light a flame against

the dark, let myself
weep. I do not

know how to pass
the border into sleep.

My body sinks

    into the cold

        hold of the water.

It's quiet
under the churn:

      barnacles and kelp, silver glint of fish,
          curve of light.

      Time collapses.

          I haven't bled for years,
            but each waxing crescent moon
              my body aches

            with cramps for a period
            that will not arrive,

              a period that's yours.

Phantom cramps, vestigial pain—
  your body, your lost present hits mine.

    I hated menstruating, hated the swell
     of your breasts,

       the blood.

The body keeps its own history.

   The pelvic pain I thought I had left behind with—

         surges within me.

    I reach up

  up to the fat sanity of the air above.

A cormorant swallows
     a silver fish whole,

               throat expanding
          with one enormous gulp.

       What wild sounds have I swallowed,

         swallowed completely?

When we were a child,
     we imagined running away,
     disguising our self as a boy.

         In our escape, we had a pet dog.

We played out this fantasy
       with a lobster buoy we found
         washed up on shore,

            dragging it behind
            our sandaled feet.

Ghost :: Persephone

I always wanted a dog,
but I never expected
this one: hound of Hades,

three shaggy heads.
He stands by the river,
allows the dead to enter

but not to leave.
I've named him
for my own, bend low

to his ear, hum lullabies
my mother used to sing
to me. He is ugly,

but he is alive: he paws
at the broken earth,
circles three times round

before he sleeps. He leans
heavy against my side,
tongues pink, panting.

Sweaty and disturbed,
Hercules dragged the dog
to the surface and back,

never asked me for permission.
Now when I go to the river,
Cerberus settles at my feet

on a pillow of moss.
Together, we watch
the dead come in.

Before we had heard the word *transgender*, how
        could we imagine

        our separation, pulling our self apart

           into *she* and *he*,

divorcing our *we*   into *you* and *I*?

        We learned how to copy our mother's voice,
           her uptilting laugh, her friendly tone.

Does my low voice now feel like a mask?

        Around most men, words leave my mouth
           short and fast.

        Still, when I answer the phone, strangers
           often call me ma'am.

(what wild sounds)

(memory cracks

open)

If Persephone was stolen by Hades into the underworld, did he take her?

If I was once a girl (you) who was taken unwillingly by a boy, did that break us?

(a boy)

(a girl)

(boy) (girl) (girl) (boy) (girl) (boy)

(what is whole)

(what is whole in the body)

(what is a hole)

(what is inviolate)

(   )

(what is missing)

(what is negation)   (what is no)

(no)   (no)   (no   no)

(no)

(hot sober breath in your ear)

(flash of ginger hair—   )

Ghost :: Persephone

I gathered flowers.

Hades poisoned me,
dragged me, t-shirt torn,

into the underland.

Poppies wilted
in my trembling hands.

Yes, of course, I screamed.

Trees can listen,
they cannot move.

I can say it now: rape.

Monster in a suit.
I would drown him

but how to destroy death

when I am lost myself
among the dead?

breathe into your Gender

allow your Gender to soften with each exhalation

hold your Gender in for a count of four

pause

let your Gender out for a count of six

repeat until your Gender starts to relax

wiggle your Gender in your fingers and your toes

keep breathing

shake your Gender with your whole body

stretch out your Gender

hold your Gender for a count of three

stick out your tongue and let your Gender release

allow your Gender to make a sound

close your eyes but keep your Gender open

rub your hands together then place them lovingly over your Gender

allow the edges of your mouth to rise as you contemplate your Gender

is your Gender still holding tension

incline your head towards your Gender

thank your Gender before you leave

In *Twelfth Night*, the two twins
      Sebastian and Viola
   are separated in a violent storm.

         They each believe the other is dead.

      Disguised as a boy, Viola renames herself Cesario, creates a new life.

Near the end of the play,
when the twins are reunited at last,
      Sebastian's friend Antonio asks:

> *How have you made division of yourself?*
> *An apple cleft in two is not more twin*
> *Than these two creatures. Which is Sebastian?*

Sebastian responds:

> *Do I stand there? I never had a brother...*
>   *I had a sister,*
> *Whom the blind waves and surges have devour'd.*

         O sister-mine, heart's twin,
           soul-mirror—

         Do I stand there?

Ghost :: Persephone

How have I made division
of myself? An apple cleft

in two, I lie where I fall.
Sometimes I pronounce

my grief aloud, howl
toward the earth, an animal

sound. Half-dead, I hollow
in the dirt. I twin myself

in shadow, I rinse
my image in the river's

shallows. I drown
my remembrance

with salt water. I was yet
of many accounted beautiful.

Full moon night. Sleep
         is impossible in the bright
                  lunar light. The ocean

                           glimmers, an invitation.
                  No lantern needed, I follow
         my choreography of life vest,

kayak, paddle. No birds
         sing this late, no songs
                  I cannot translate.

                           I crest over the waves
                  toward the horizon.
         With each paddle stroke

the water glows: bioluminescent
         plankton create blue swirls
                  of sparkling light. Twin

                           whispers of moon and sea
                  pull me on a simple line
         to the sea cave, entrance

to your world. My heart?
         Deadweight, warning
                  me to turn around—

                           I do not listen. Instead,
                  I flow through the booming
         entrance, turn my back on

the prophet-moon. I bow
         into the tunnel's tight pinch,
                  fold my body into the unknown

                           scream of earth
                  and hidden light.

can you see
here in the underworld
my vision plays tricks on me
I peer into
a turquoise lake
a downy blue of stars above
phosphorescent swirl below
knuckles scraped on rock
a kind of magic
so burn sage
and breathe
send
skyward
to the night
grief or
strange light
and see only
you
my ghost
my sister
reflection of my
past
you call to me
as time collapses
into our one body
alive in an
aubade of
the animal
starlit
thorn-caught
a fracturing of
the poet or
a mirror
smashed into
shards of
hidden
witness
a story
out of history

my body
like a dream
in this half-light
a cavern which holds
a vast space
glow worms pulse on the walls
a soft blue light
a trickle of blood
there is no science
burn cedar
in the flame
a prayer
through rock
like a door into
a mirror
I look upon
you
my lost
self
my brother
future
or present
come closer
as time unfolds
singing itself
electric
metamorphosis
the wild one
within
we break open
identity
Persephone
the moon
lunar fractals
light
within us
a risen text
we spool
into myth

I lied earlier,

when I said I returned the seal's body to the sea.

The truth is—

What happened was—

In fact, I—

I glided over turquoise water,

beached my kayak on the creamy sand,

saw the dead seal

and turned away.

I walked through beach roses

to the island's windward side.

Looked out over the frothing surf,
smoked a joint, laid out in the sun,
read a book for a while.

Sun-parched, I returned to the beach:
the tide had risen, the body

had disappeared.

Wind whipped the waves

whitecapped and rough.

As I started toward home,

struggling against the surf,

I glanced back and thought—

it was hard to tell—

the seal's still body—

Did you see it too?

A little to the left of the beach,   on the ledge?

Were those rib bones

or just striations in the stones?

I'm beginning to recognize
    the birds I see here:
        the loud chortle

            of the laughing gull,
      the red crest and heavy bill
of the pileated woodpecker

who wings by while I
    sip coffee on the deck.
        A hermit thrush sounds

            out mournfully on grey
      mornings. You memorized
bird songs one lazy

summer, so it feels
    as though I'm recalling
        a lost language. I hear

            the forest differently
      when I can understand
who's here with me.

Ghost :: Persephone

I sing a charm
of goldfinches,

a field of wildflowers
in full bloom, a slap

of wings on water.
Listen for my hum

in the slow stretch of the pines,
the ocean's steady breath.

You do not have to abandon
your sweet self

to love what is lost.
I'll never be sorry.

Inverted flower, open
        the fig to reveal
                a seeded galaxy

                        amid a whirl
                of flesh. Each fig
        is a womb, a tomb

for the fig wasp,
        the female who
                crawls inside,

                        loses her wings
                and antennae
        in the tight squeeze.

She lays her eggs
        then dies. Follow
                the cycle: offspring

                        mate, wingless
                males bite through
        the flesh, the sisters

wriggle out, fly.

our Gender is many feathered

                                                        our Gender is a living thing

                        our Gender slides around

                                        expands

                our Gender is our own

                                                    our Gender is reflective

                                                        refracting

                                                heavy leaded

    our Gender is galactic

                        our Gender howls and barks

                        our Gender is difficult to hold

                                                    our Gender is delicate

                                                hollow-boned

                    our Gender is about to take flight

Think jump.

Flight.

The geometry of air.

A storm off the coast.
        Strange tides pull in
                sprawling brown seaweed

                        tangled with birthday
                balloons, charred logs,
        the thick rubber bands

used to bind lobster
        claws, bottles and cans,
                dead horseshoe crabs.

                        I paddle around
                the island, pass under
        the drawbridge at the gut,

that tight cinch of water
        between the island
                and the mainland.

                        By the fishermen's co-op,
                the surprise of a great blue
        heron, its long legs balancing

on a raft by a stack
        of lobster traps. It eyes
                me through one yellow

                        iris then the next.
                Shakes out its feathers
        then soars to the shore.

My ghost, sister-self, after all this time

I still don't know what pronouns to use for you,

for me, for us.

Are we one or two?

Am I an *I* and you a *you*?

When I was young was I myself my *I*, or was I *you*?

Or were we a *we*, plural in our
intertwined yet also singular self?

I don't know.

We elude easy definition.

Sometimes I miss your soprano,

the smooth skin of your face,

a softness I lack.

Sometimes I almost forget how you existed.

Yet always I feel you tight within,

a second heartbeat

inside my chest.

Ghost :: Persephone

When I swim out
the moon hangs luminously
where it should

as if awaiting me.
Each return, a reckoning.
Seal-like, I haul

my rose of a body
onto the rocky shore,
salt-licked and heaving.

The cottage still
overlooks the mirror sea.
I climb the cliff

toward the yellow
kitchen, warmed
by the woodstove.

Now the worn
linoleum reminds me
only of itself: optimistic

floral pattern scrubbed thin.
You clatter cream
into coffee, an offering.

We breathe the blessed
air together, blood
fluttering in our veins.

Notes

This book is indebted to the trans poets who have come before me. The conceit of writing to a younger or alternate not-trans self was inspired by TC Tolbert's "Dear Melissa:" poems and Samuel Ace's epistolary introduction to *Meet Me There: Normal Sex & Home in three days. Don't wash.* (Belladonna* Series, 2019) in which Ace writes, "Dear friend who is me and no longer me, dear love who I have never left behind, dear gorgeous *Linda*, in all that your name implies, let me say again that I love you." The tenderness of this address broke something open in me and made this book that you hold in your hands possible.

My obsession with caves, the underworld, and the myth of Persephone was kindled and informed by three central texts: Louise Glück's *Averno* (Farrar, Straus and Giroux, 2006), Robert Macfarlane's *Underland: a deep time journey* (W. W. Norton & Company, 2019), and Edith Hamilton's *Mythology: Timeless Tales of Gods and Heroes* (Little Brown and Company, 1942).

The setting of this book is an imagined island in mid-coast Maine. Monhegan Island, Damariscove Island, and Rutherford Island were all key inspirations for this location.

The use of the double colon was inspired by Dane Slutzky's poem "Call to Adventure," published online by Zócalo Public Square (April 9, 2021). Other inspirations for the use of the double colon include evie shockley's collection *semiautomatic* (Wesleyan University Press, 2017) and Brian Teare's collection *Doomstead Days* (Nightboat Books, 2019). I think of the double colon as a doorway, a hinge, a way of holding two ideas in tandem.

"*Ghost :: Persephone* The inky black of the mantilla" borrows the phrase "Shut as a seashell" from the poem "Lady Lazarus," authored by Sylvia Plath in *Ariel* (Faber and Faber, 1965), which reads "I rocked shut // As a seashell."

The italicized Gender poems are in conversation with the explorations of the word "gender" in the poem "Doomstead Days" authored by Brian Teare in *Doomstead Days* (Nightboat Books, 2019).

"A dense fog descends" refers to the 2020 El Dorado fire in California, allegedly started by a couple using a smoke bomb to reveal the gender of their soon-to-be-born baby.

The italicized lines in "In *Twelfth Night*, the two twins" are taken from Act 5, scene 1 in William Shakespeare's *Twelfth Night*: Act 5.1.218-220 and Act 5.1.222-225.

"*Ghost :: Persephone* How have I made division" is in conversation with *Twelfth Night*. The final lines "I drown / my remembrance // with salt water. I was yet / of many accounted beautiful" are in reference to Act 2, scene 2, in which Sebastian describes his lost twin sister: "A lady, sir, though it was said she much / resembled me, was yet of many accounted beautiful. / But though I could not with such estimable wonder / over-far believe that, yet thus far I will boldly publish / her: she bore a mind that envy could not but call fair. / She is drowned already, sir, with salt water, though I / seem to drown her remembrance again with more" (Act 2.1.23-29).

Publication Acknowledgments

These poems originally appeared in the following journals and publications, occasionally in different forms, often with different titles:

Birdcoat Quarterly: "By mid-summer, lobster buoys" published as "ghost traps" and "*Ghost :: Persephone* When I want to feel" published as "Was I once called Persephone?"

Broadsided Press: "can you see" published as "Letter With My Ghost"

Cobra Milk: "(what wild sounds)" and "(a boy)" published as "Hades"

The Columbia Review: "*Ghost :: Persephone* How have I made division of myself?" published as "Devoured"

The Common: "Bound by rocky headlands," "Buoyed by the salt water," and "Here in the one place" published as "To My Ghost :: Float."

Diode Poetry Journal: "I wake up before dawn," "*Ghost :: Persephone* You and I both know," and "Full moon night" published as "The Sea Cave" and "*Ghost :: Persephone* I name each day" published as "dead name"

Driftwood Press Literary Magazine: "Did our division begin" and "In *Twelfth Night*, the two twins" published as "An Apple Cleft in Two"

Four Way Review: "Inverse twin, lost sister," "Where do we converge," and "Every Sunday I pierce my thigh" published as "inverse twin, lost sister" and "*Ghost :: Persephone* I have no answers" published as "Persephone, am I the pomegranate and you the seed?"

Leon Literary Review: "*Ghost :: Persephone* I always wanted a dog" published as "Persephone & Cerberus" and "*Ghost :: Persephone* When I swim out" published as "Persephone, Spring"

Riddle Fence: "Your Gender is a punk house party" published as "Gender Diagram II"

Salamander Magazine: "I find comfort in the rhythm" published as "to the girl who once was me" and "breathe into your Gender," published as "Gender Diagram VI"

wildness: "Girl-ghost" published as "To My Ghost"

Personal Acknowledgments

Thank you to Kimiko Hahn for seeing worth in these pages and for selecting *GHOST :: SEEDS* for publication with Texas Review Press.

To J. Bruce Fuller, Karisma "Charlie" Tobin, and everyone at Texas Review Press for your support and vision in bringing this book to print.

To Zoe Schlacter for designing the cover of my dreams and to Beowulf Sheehan for an author portrait that made me feel truly seen.

The 2022-23 Larry Levis Post-Graduate Stipend from Friends of Writers provided critical support of this work.

To the teachers and mentors who have believed in and guided my writing: Frank Bidart, Stephanie Burt, Gaby Calvocoressi, Dan Chiasson, Timothy Donnelly, Sally Keith, Patricia Lothrop, Alex Myers, Paul Tran, and Mark Wunderlich.

To Emily Nemens, Craig Morgan Teicher, and Robin Jones for your mentorship and support during my time as a reader for *The Paris Review*.

Deep gratitude to Ellen Bryant Voigt for introducing me to the MFA Program for Writers at Warren Wilson College and to Debra Allbery, Kaveh Akbar, Christine Kitano, Jason Schneiderman, Connie Voisine, and Alan Williamson for your instruction and guidance. Thank you to Friends of Writers and to David Lanier for the Rodney Jack Scholarship.

To the Bread Loaf Writers' Conference, Tin House Winter Workshop, and the Juniper Summer Writing Institute for providing inspiration, community, and support.

To Lizzy Beck, Eric Cruz, Emmi Greer, Daniela Naomi Molnar, Sebastián Páramo, Megan Pinto, Dane Slutzky, and Jason Storms for reading early versions of this manuscript and offering generous editorial feedback. Thank you also to Sebastián Páramo for helping me title this work.

To my parents John and Martha for your love and your willingness to learn and grow with me. So much gratitude and love to my grandparents Jeanne and Larry and to my entire extended family for the gift of space and time to write in our family cottage on the Maine coast.

To my beloved husband Dane: thank you for being my best and first reader, for believing in me, and for supporting my writing in every way that matters. Thank you to puppy Daphne and cat Bear for reminding me of the importance of rest, snuggles, and long walks.

To trans people everywhere: I wouldn't be here without you. This book is for you.

About the Author

Sebastian Merrill was the 2022-23 winner of the Levis Prize for Poetry from Friends of Writers and he was selected as a member of the 2023 Get the Word Out inaugural poetry cohort for debut writers from *Poets & Writers*. A staff-scholar for the Bread Loaf Writers' Conference in 2022 and 2023, Sebastian has also received support from Tin House Workshop and the Juniper Summer Writing Institute. The recipient of the Rodney Jack Scholarship from Friends of Writers, he holds an MFA in Poetry from Warren Wilson College and a BA in English Literature, Creative Writing, and South Asian Studies from Wellesley College.

2022 Winner of The X. J. Kennedy Poetry Prize

Selected by Kimiko Hahn

Established in 1998, The X. J. Kennedy Prize highlights one full-length collection of poetry per year.

PREVIOUS WINNERS:

Kathleen Rooney, *Where Are the Snows*
Brooke Sahni, *Before I Had the Word*
Caroline M. Mar, *Special Education*
Garret Keizer, *The World Pushes Back*
Jay Udall, *Because a Fire in Our Heads*
Jeff Hardin, *No Other Kind of World*
Gwen Hart, *The Empress of Kisses*
Corinna McClanahan Schroeder, *Inked*
Ashley Mace Havird, *The Garden of the Fugitives*
Jeff Worley, *A Little Luck*